TWINSOME MINDS

AN ACT OF DOUBLE REMEMBRANCE

RICHARD KEARNEY
& SHEILA GALLAGHER

This essay is part of the interdisciplinary series *Famine Folios*, covering many aspects of the Great Hunger in Ireland from 1845–52.

CONTENTS

Cover | Hughie O'Donoghue, *On Our Knees*

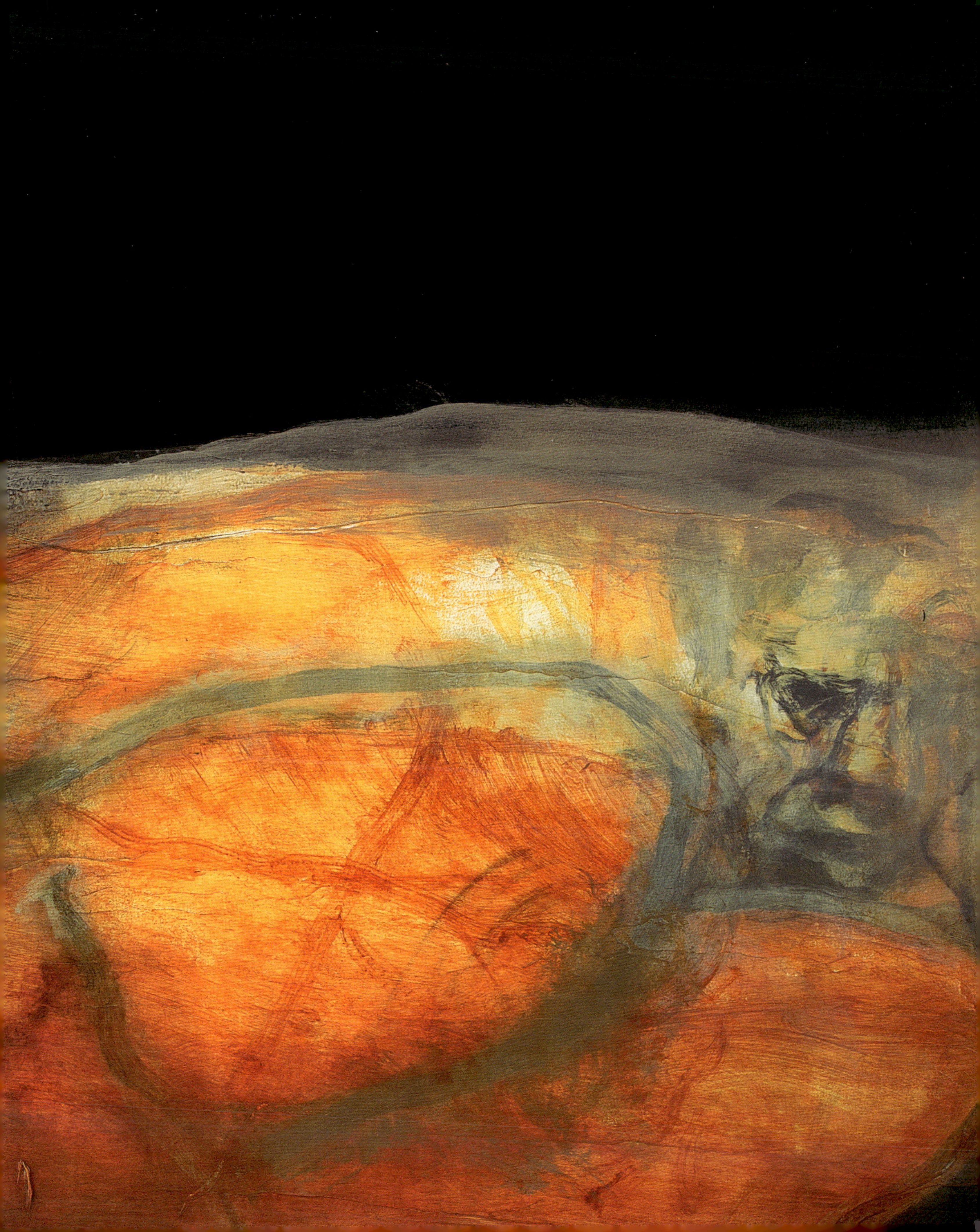

PREFATORY NOTE

This folio is a published version of a multimedia performance staged in fifteen cities in Europe and North America in 2016 to commemorate the hundredth anniversary of the Easter Rising in Dublin **[Figure 1]**. Our hope is that the double medium of word and image may provide a creative and therapeutic means of representing the trauma of 1916, and of the Famine that ghosted it. As recent trauma studies reveal, the "unexperienced experiences" of trauma return first as images and then as words. The images in this volume are based on various kinds of representation used by Sheila Gallagher in the live performance, including original ink drawings, archival photographs, and stills from digital projections. The stories by Richard Kearney take the form of micro-narratives of both oral and written history. We hope to honor both media of recovery – visual and textual – in this folio presentation.

We are very grateful to the following people for making *Twinsome Minds* see the light of day on stage and now in print and video: Kevin Sweet, our brilliant and indispensable technical director; Fiach Mac Conghail, director of the Abbey Theatre in Dublin, who first commissioned the performance and organized its world premiere at the National Theatre of Ireland, Dublin in January 2016; Ambassador Anne Anderson and Ciaran Walsh, who facilitated major funding through Culture Ireland; the Institute of Liberal Arts and the Irish Studies Program at Boston College for their generous pre-production and post-production support; Elizabeth Shannon and the Shannon Fellowship at Boston University for sponsoring the Tsai performance in Boston; and the following great colleagues and friends who served as creative collaborators and consultants at various stages of the work's development from proposal to stage, print, and film: Robert Savage, Fanny Howe, Brian O'Donovan, Roy Foster, Declan Kiberd, Claire Wills, John Peto, John Horgan, Mary Jones, Cathal Stephens, Louise Callaghan, Ronan Sheehan, Luke Gibbons, Diarmuid Ferriter, Simon Sleeman, Deb Todd Wheeler, Matthew Littell, Scott Cummings, Seán McGrath, Brian Treanor, James Taylor, Goncalo Marcello, Marta Ceia, Anne Bernard, James Murphy, Orla O'Hanrahan, and Nora Hickey.

A special thanks finally to Niamh O'Sullivan and Grace Brady of Ireland's Great Hunger Museum for their expert and gracious shepherding of our manuscript to completion at Quinnipiac University Press.

Figure 1 | Sheila Gallagher, *Twinsome Minds: Ferdia and Cuchulain*

1916 AND THE FAMINE

1916 was not just about 1916. It was also about other events before and after. Events real and imagined, spoken and unspoken, remembered and unremembered. From the mythic death of Cuchulain and the great Book of Invasions down to the 1798 Rebellion, the Fenian Revolt, and the terrible Famine of the 1840s. Such formative traumas would find voice again in the historic 1916 Rising. The great ruptures and calamities of Ireland's tragic history would, many 1916 rebels believed, be at last redeemed. The Proclamation of the Irish Republic said as much. It summoned the Irish people to rise up in the name of lost generations and fight for liberty. "In the name of God and of the dead generations from which she receives her old tradition of nationhood, Ireland, through us, summons her children to her flag and strikes for freedom." The signatories appealed to a transgenerational legacy of suffering and struggle, where the forgotten victims of history could be revived in a glorious act of emancipation for future generations. It was a classic feat of "anticipatory memory".[1] And by this double solicitation of the fatefully deceased and those still to come, it claimed to break open historical time to a more mythic time: a time where "all the children of the nation", past and future, could be cherished equally.

Pádraig Pearse, the leader of the Rising, had already invoked the dead in his famous graveside oration for Jeremiah O'Donovan Rossa in 1915. Here he spoke of new life rising from the graves of "dead generations" (the same phrase used in the Proclamation). Speaking "in spiritual communion" with these ancestral ghosts of the past, he declared that "life springs from death"; and he was surely not unmindful of the forty thousand souls who perished of hunger during the Famine some seventy years before in a town closely associated with O'Donovan Rossa, Skibbereen. Indeed, Pearse's own grandparents lived through the national catastrophe. The forgotten victims of the "bad times" (*an drochshaol*) would surely be amongst those redeemed in the sacrificial martyrdom of the Easter Rising. The time for the insurrection was planned for Easter Sunday as a day of holy resurrection: a miraculous moment when Ireland's "ghosts" might return as "ancestors" and give birth to a new, independent Ireland. As Pearse put it, "from the graves of ... [the dead] spring living nations ... and while Ireland holds these graves, Ireland unfree shall never be at peace" (Pádraig Pearse oration at the funeral of Jeremiah O'Donovan Rossa, August 1915).

It is surprising that Pearse – and other 1916 leaders – did not identify the Famine as a direct cause of the rebellion. This omission is surely symptomatic of an unconscious repression of inherited trauma. For trauma it certainly was: the loss of over one million to disease and starvation in 1845–46, the forced exile of another two million in the following decade, and the near decimation of Ireland's native Gaelic culture, thereafter banished to the meager extremities of the western seaboard. As Michael D. Higgins notes: "The Irish Famine of 1845–50 was the greatest social disaster – in terms of mortality and suffering – that Ireland has ever experienced. It was also the worst social calamity based on crop failure ever experienced in Europe, indeed in the 'developed' word, in modern times"(55). What Higgins calls the desperate "struggle for an adequate term" was evident in the lack of commonly accredited memories, narratives, or names for the Famine for the immediate generations of survivors: instead, a loose variety of stand-ins were used in both languages: *an gorta*, *an drochshaol*, the hunger, the calamity, the bad times, Black '47, and so forth. While it is true that a few protagonists of the Rising – notably Roger Casement, James Connolly, and Maud Gonne – were shocked by the brutal horror of the Famine, even they made no explicit causal connection between it and the Rising.[2] No one spoke of the rebellion as an act of defiance or revenge against the empire that had sanctioned such unspeakable wrong. Yet who could deny that the ruins of abandoned Famine villages ghosted the rubble of Dublin after 1916. To juggle with poet Seamus Deane, the hunger in their bones erupted in stones.

Unspeakable was the operative word. The Famine was an experience of brutal truncation – a moment that aborted the development of Irish cultural history, dividing it into before and after. Like all great traumas it was an "unexperienced experience" that could not be represented or explained at the time, but would have to await generations before being memorialized and "worked through".[3] The only viable response of survivors was, to echo James Joyce, "silence, exile and cunning" (the latter expressing itself in the adage "Whatever you say, say nothing"). Emily Lawless, writing of the Famine at the turn of the twentieth century, ruefully observed that the most visible mark of the event was its invisibility – no more than a few derelict Famine roads and ghost villages, which were quickly forgotten. Unclaimed and abandoned. Roofless disappearing ruins **[Figure 2]**, "futile and abortive". Lawless writes of "wrecks of cabins ... [with] nettles spreading across their hearthstones ... the last traces of what was once a populous village, without so much as a *hic jacet* to say where it stood" (37). Traumatised silence mixed with survivor guilt and the need to forget. The Famine destroyed the very instruments that might have measured it. The Rising was a delayed response, seventy years *après coup*. A return of the repressed.

We may say then that the links between the Great Hunger and 1916 were less articulated than acted out, less acknowledged than performed. One moved from an act of rupture involuntarily endured (the Famine) to one voluntarily enacted (the Rising). For, make no mistake, most of the 1916 leaders knew very well they were heading for martyrdom, for glorious failure. And willed it so. "We came here

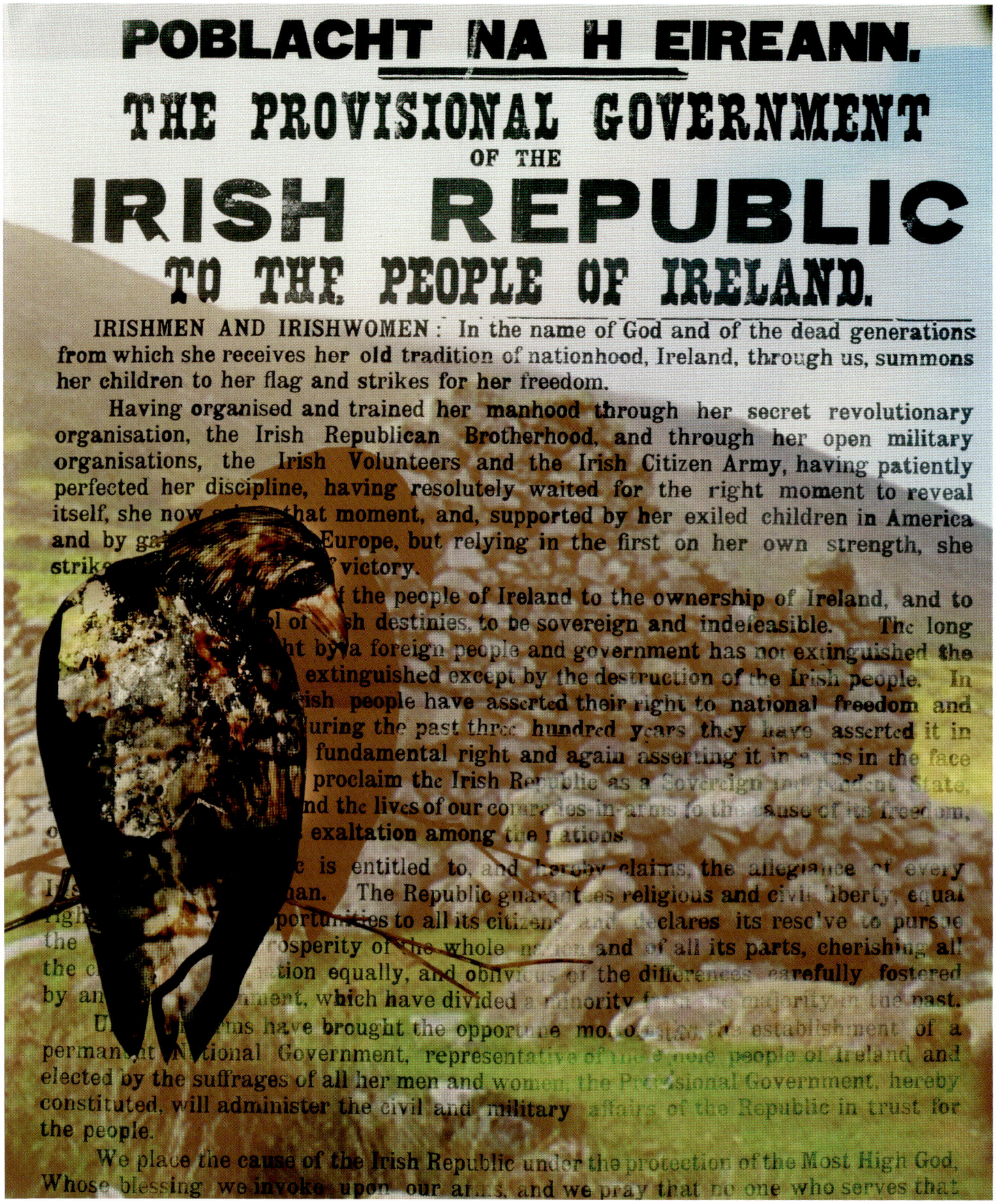
POBLACHT NA H EIREANN.
THE PROVISIONAL GOVERNMENT
OF THE
IRISH REPUBLIC
TO THE PEOPLE OF IRELAND.
IRISHMEN AND IRISHWOMEN: In the name of God and of the dead generations
from which she receives her old tradition of nationhood, Ireland, through us, summons
her children to her flag and strikes for her freedom.
Having organised and trained her manhood through her secret revolutionary
organisation, the Irish Republican Brotherhood, and through her open military
organisations, the Irish Volunteers and the Irish Citizen Army, having patiently
perfected her discipline, having resolutely waited for the right moment to reveal

Figure 2 | Sheila Gallagher, *From the Graves Spring*

not to win but to lose", as one rebel leader avowed, anticipating hunger-striker Terence MacSwiney's declaration three years later: "It is not those who inflict the greatest suffering but those who endure it who will win in the end."[4] This was a logic of sacrificial suffering that – mixing the Celtic Cuchulain with the messianic Christ – triggered an unconscious "repetition" of traumas, seeking to transform the calamitous past into a new future. Elements of unpredictability, impossibility, shock, and surprise informed both events: the traumatic ruin of Ireland's Gaelic population being replicated in the traumatic oblation of the Dublin rebels. The Famine split between victim and survivor foreshadowed the 1916 split between Irish/ British siblings. Following the unconscious logic of repetition, the Easter ritual of redemptive violence might miraculously salvage the unbearable, unnamable loss of the "bad times". Its cathartic drama might turn executed victims into national heroes, the crucified into the risen. And so it was greeted by many over time. By 1922, just six years after the Rising, most of Ireland had become a free, independent state.

In the process it is arguable that leaders of the new nation compensated for the non-remembering of the Famine with an over-remembering of the Rising. Grand narratives of myth and martyrdom quickly dwarfed the little stories of ordinary Irish men and women who had experienced the complex pain and confusion of 1916 first hand, both during Easter Week in Dublin and on the battlefields of Belgium and France, where thousands of Irish died at Ypres and the Somme that same year. In short, under-commemoration of Famine victims (in the nineteenth century) became hyper-commemoration of martyred heroes (in the twentieth). This was an understandable strategy of compensation for a people humiliated by imperial hegemony and deprived of the "work of memory" necessary for genuine mourning.[5] Yet something was lost in the often compulsive and ritualistic hyperbole of the repetition: namely, the "reality principle" of ordinary human lives, the memory of common brothers and sisters in arms who expired in the ruins of Dublin and the Somme.

In an attempt to temper this mood swing of memory and forgetting, we offer here some stories and images occluded by the binary dualisms of official history, Irish and British. Responding to the traumatic legacy of breaking and splitting, we propose a sample of micro-narratives that disclose a logic of both/and rather than either/or. And so doing we endeavor, symbolically, to transform "melancholy into mourning", turning the repetition-backwards of trauma into a repetition-forwards of drama. In short, our presentation is a modest attempt to address what Dori Laub calls the "failure of witnessing".[6]

TEXT BY RICHARD KEARNEY | IMAGES BY SHEILA GALLAGHER

BETWEEN HISTORY AND STORY

To begin on a personal note. In 1966 I made a scrapbook of the 1916 heroes **[Figure 3]**. Like most other schoolchildren in the Irish Republic, I was celebrating the fiftieth anniversary of the Rising. I presented the book to my teacher, Brother O'Reilly, in Christian Brothers College, Cork, and received a silver coin of Pádraig Pearse **[Figure 4]** in return. Half a century later, much has changed and my goal is different: not, this time, to recount grand narratives of the Great Irish Martyrs but to look at some little narratives largely neglected by history.

In west Cork there is a saying: "If you want to know what happened, ask your father; if you want to know what people *say* happened, ask your mother." In this volume we hope to ask both questions by revisiting certain "sites of memory" where history and story overlap. Histories tell things that happened, stories things that *might* have happened. Where history stops, stories start. For, as novelist Roddy Doyle says, we need stories to fill the hole inside us. In what follows we'll be trying to fill in some gaps of history by supplementing memory with imagination, by telling it both *as* it happened and *as if* it happened in this way or that. For it's often in mixing history and story that we give a future to the past.

1916 was a great rising and a great sundering – between Ireland and Britain, north and south, nationalist and unionist. There are two ways of reliving that split: either as recurring division or as a chance to create something new. One way of recreating the past is by retrieving forgotten tales of opposite sides – two nations, two places, two persons, two parts of ourselves – and transforming the tensions into novel modes of imagining.

1916 was a revolution of mind as well as might. It was as much about cultural imagination as it was about military insurrection. In the 2016 centenary of the Rising, Ireland witnessed many military commemorations, but sometimes forgot that half the 1916 leaders were poets and that the revolutionary generation that gave birth to the Rising teemed with artists and intellectuals, painters and playwrights, writers and storytellers. It is important to move beyond martial gun salutes and recover, in Yeats's

Figure 3 | 1916 commemoration scrapbook (fiftieth anniversary, 1966)

words, the "Ireland the poets have imagined" ("The Municipal Gallery Revisited", 1937).

Militarist memory easily ignores just how complex 1916 was, particularly for those who lived it. The same year that saw almost five hundred die in the Rising saw 3,500 Irish die at the Battle of the Somme in a single day. This was a time of massive confusion, and it is not fair to remember one part of Ireland's family without remembering the other – namely, *both* the Irish Volunteers who fought *against* Britain, *and* the Royal Irish Fusiliers who fought *with* Britain. It means honoring the Easter lily symbolizing those who died in Dublin, *and* the red poppy symbolizing those who died in Flanders. It means acknowledging what the Irish writer Seán Ó Faoláin called the "Siamese duality of mind" epitomizing British–Irish history.

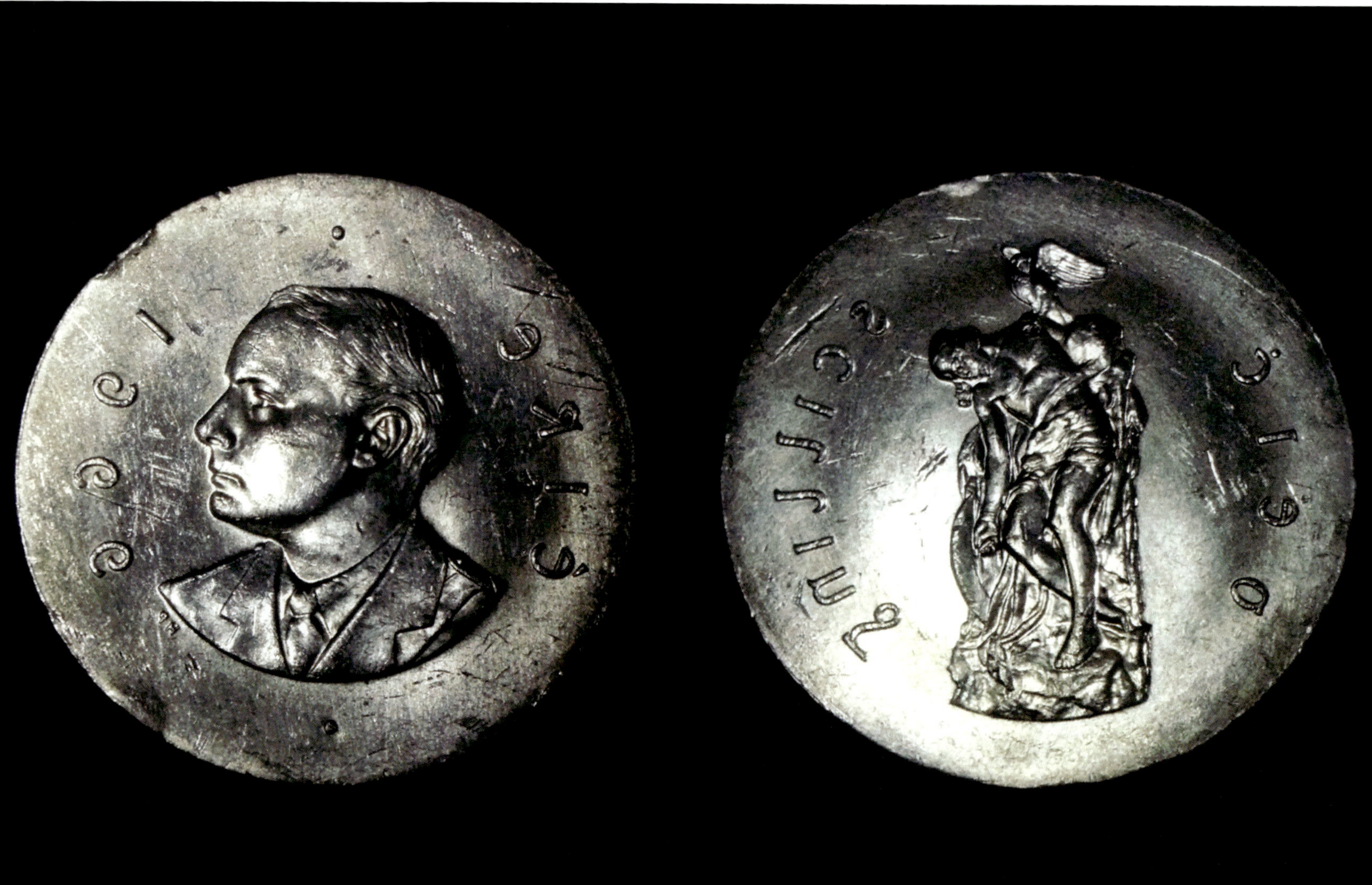

James Joyce argued that Irish imagination was at its best when moving between two "twinsome" minds – that is, when it had "two thinks at a time". The Irish were always most creative when following a logic of *both/and*, acknowledging a mix of double fidelities: religious, national, psychological, cultural – doublings that call for new mediations. Ireland is an island beside an island, part of an archipelago connected by waterways that make us all "mongrel islanders". "We are what we are, mongrel pure", Thomas Kinsella wryly observed ("Butcher's Dozen", 1972). And his contemporary Seamus Heaney put it well regarding his own dual upbringing on the Irish border: "two buckets were easier carried than one, I grew up in between" ("Terminus", 1987). The key is this *between* that summons what Heaney called a "symbolic reordering of Ireland" open to new possibilities of "Irishness, Britishness, Europeaness, planitariness, creatureliness, whatever". For "whatever is given/can always be reimagined" (Heaney 200).

The philosophy of "twinsome minds" seeks to turn polar opposites into fertile openings. It is a way of thinking that informed the Good Friday Agreement of 1998, ultimately sanctioned by both British and Irish governments: a peace agreement that took the gun out of Irish politics by allowing people to be "Irish or British or *both*". That document, like the 1916 Proclamation itself, is still a promissory note – and one needs to make good on such promises rather than settle for stop-gap solutions. (There are still, shockingly, over eighty so-called "peace walls" separating communities in Northern Ireland along purely sectarian lines, and almost eighty per cent of education remains religiously segregated. War wounds fester south of the border, too.)

As a symbolic gesture beyond such divides, we offer here some images and stories of people who "grew up in between" – tales of crossed identity often eclipsed by "monumental history". The true enemies of commemoration are not complexity and confusion but purity and certitude. As Brian Friel reminds us in his play *Translations* (1980), "confusion is not an ignoble condition". Genuine catharsis comes from a *crossing* of narratives, transforming binaries into multiple belongings. It is important, we believe, to complicate and pluralise the memory of 1916 with new gestures of imagination.

Figure 4 | **Pádraig Pearse 1966 commemorative coin**

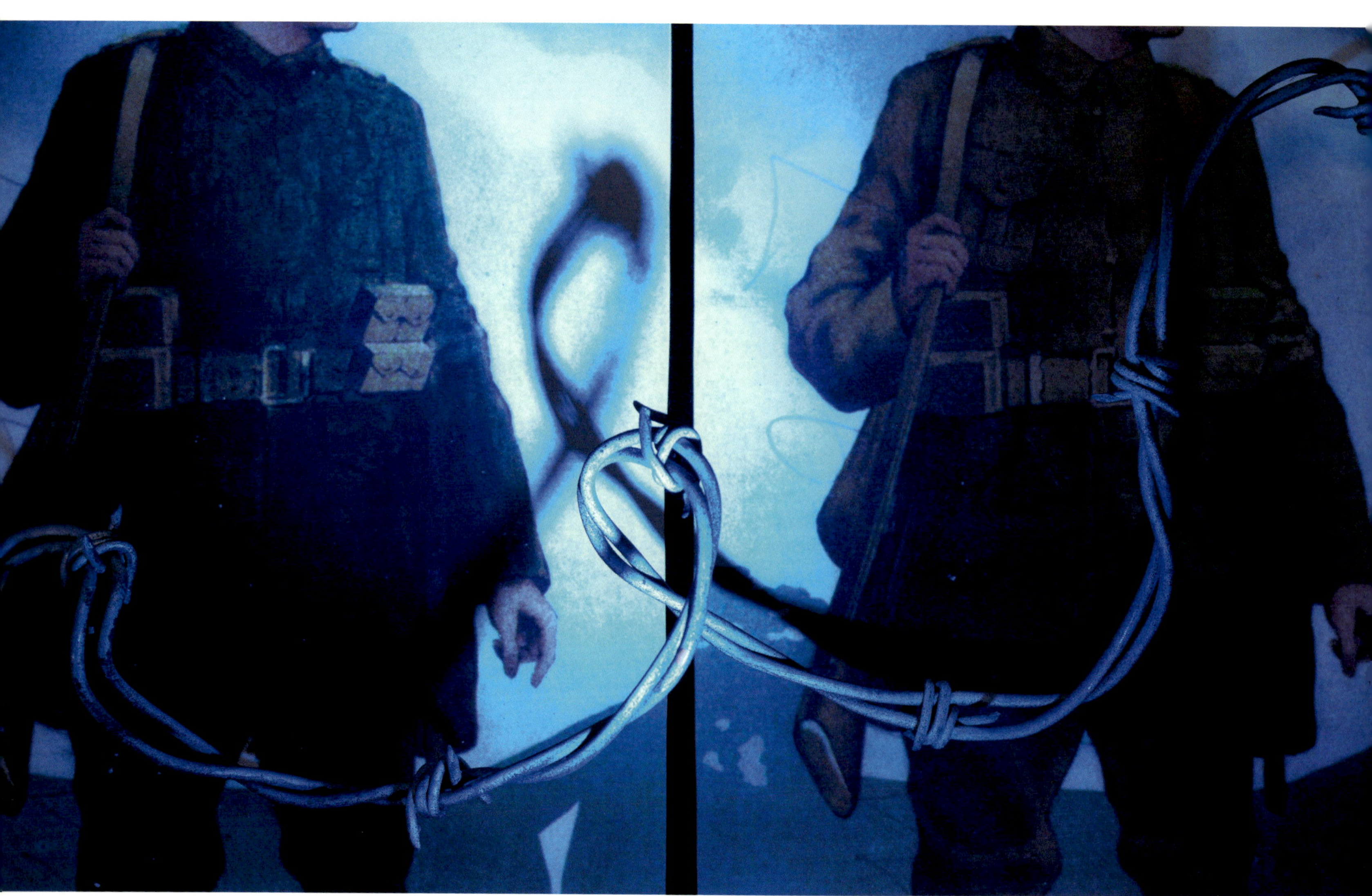

SPLIT SIBLINGS

We begin with stories of split siblings caught on opposite sides in 1916.

I

Cyril and William Stevens were born within fourteen months of each other in Fermanagh, and ended up in rival armies in 1916. Cyril joined the rebels, while William, a soldier in the British army, found himself guarding his own brother in a Dublin jail. One week after the Rising, they stared at each other across barbed wire. The uniforms they wore – Irish and British – were made by the same Dublin tailor **[Figure 5]**. Same wool, same stripes, same buttons, same braid; only the color was different: Olive green for Cyril, dun brown for William.

There is a photograph of their reunion with their sister in 1946, two months before Cyril died – the last time they met.

II

Another example involved siblings from the north of Ireland. Fervently Protestant, George and William Irving became lovers of Gaelic and all things Irish. One day they saw two posters on a wall, one promising an Irish Republic, the other recruiting for "King and Country". Both called for the defense of "small nations" (namely, Ireland and Belgium). William read the former, George the latter. They shook hands, wished each other well and went their separate ways. On May 11, 1916 a unionist paper, the *Impartial Reporter*, ran the headline "An Enniskillen traitor", denouncing George Irvine as a "rebel" in the Rising. But the paper had got the wrong brother. It was in fact William who fought in the rebellion, while George was serving in Flanders, protecting his British unit from German artillery. George loved his brother to the end, and his passion for the teaching of Gaelic, according to his sister, never "impaired his usefulness, either as a teacher or a soldier".

Figure 5 | Sheila Gallagher, *Same Wool*

III

A third story concerns blood brothers who switched uniforms during the Rising. On Easter Monday Eoin Creuss Callaghan returned from England to his native Dublin. A twenty-year-old Catholic serving in the British Air Corps, he'd been granted leave to visit his dying mother. He was wearing a British uniform and got caught in the crossfire. As it happened, a rebel sniper rescued him, took him to safety in the Four Courts, and exchanged uniforms. Next day Eoin crossed the Liffey and visited his mother for the last time. The sniper who rescued him was, the story goes, a Dublin school friend he'd sat beside for years.

Just days after his return to England, Eoin Callaghan's plane was shot down by the Germans **[Figure 6]**. *Ar dheis Dé go raibh a anam dílis.* Three generations later, his granddaughter, poet Louise Callaghan, wrote a verse called "School Yearbook" about a tale untold for almost a century:

I keep turning to his photo ... A boy soldier
Home on leave. His last look.
The story goes of him arrested,
Held over Easter in the Four Courts.
Ice winds ploughing up the Liffey.
Insurgents as young as himself,
Among ruins, crouched in a door.
Any one of them could be
From his class in school.
The contradictory clatter of war
Sounding off the cobbled quays.

Figure 6 | Sheila Gallagher, *Eoin Callaghan's Plane*

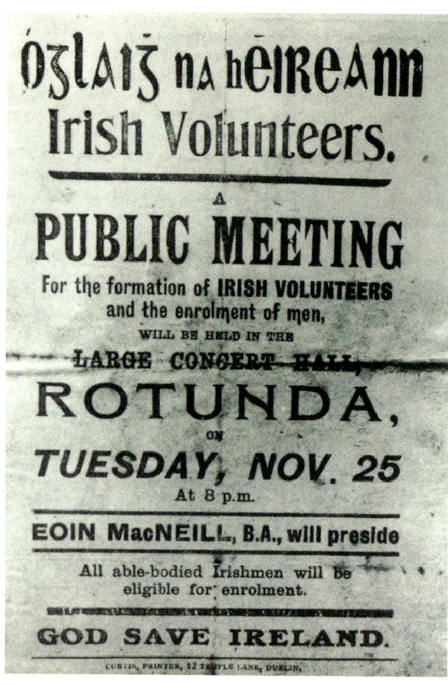

Figure 7 | Irish Volunteers and First World War recruitment posters

TRANSGENERATIONAL MEMORY

These stories of forgotten figures were recovered by descendants generations later. There are thousands of such examples all over Ireland – families split between dual loyalties – including members of my own Irish-nationalist family whose education was paid for by a British navy pension! In fact I believe that most people in Ireland who scratch their ancestral skin will uncover similar tales. This work of transgenerational memory remains a critical therapeutic task today. It matters for the health of the nation. Any nation. Why? Because repressed wounds scar the psyche and return to haunt us again and again. Such wounds need to be constantly reworked in images and words.

Revisiting micro-stories of 1916, one is struck by the contingency of events. The Rising took many by surprise, and most were at the mercy of the moment. The majority of participants, on both sides, had no real clue what would result from their actions. So much depended on chance – what street poster you read **[Figure 7]**, what uniform you chose, what message you believed: the Irish Volunteers, under Pearse, promising independence from Britain, or the National Volunteers, under Redmond, urging solidarity with Britain against Germany. And one must not forget that *both* armies – rebel and British – were committed to providing well for soldiers' families. (One should not underestimate the importance of British army salaries for the families of the 200,000 Irishmen who fought in the First World War. And the Irish Volunteers also cared for their own, with assistance from labor unions at home and abroad, including the American mining unions of Pennsylvania and New England).

It is also relevant to recall that both Irish nationalists and unionists claimed the same mythic hero – Cuchulain – as their patron. A double claim witnessed to this day in the gable murals of divided Ulster ghettos.

The fact is that, in the hierarchical days of 1916, ordinary Irish and British soldiers were told little enough by their own leaders, and even the leaders themselves were frequently at odds: think of the conflicting commands by Pearse and MacNeill at the outbreak of the Rising, not to mention the muddling in the British high command. No wonder half the troops were bemused. Nothing confounds like war. There is even the tale of Dublin Fusiliers shooting at members of a British unit who were firing at women stealing bread from Boland's mills. The British authorities accused rebels of the shooting rather than admit to mutiny in their own ranks.

But if there was confusion in the streets of Dublin, it was worse in the trenches of Flanders. Private Willie Dunne in Sebastian Barry's novel *The Long Way Home* (2005) captures this in an exchange with fellow Fusilier Captain O'Hara. They have just received news of the Dublin executions and realize that their compatriots were not only firing at British uniforms like theirs but, worse, were shipping arms from Germany!

"The queer thing is," said O'Hara, "the queer thing is, they were hoping the fucking Germans would help them."
"Who, Pete?" said Willie.
"The fucking rebels, Willie."
"Oh yeh, I know," said Willie. "I know. Sure it was written on their piece of paper. Gallant allies in Europe, it said, wasn't it?"
"So that means, like it or lump it, we're the fucking enemy. I mean, we're the fucking enemy of the fucking rebels!"
"That's it, more or less. That's how I understand it anyhow," said Willie.
"You see, I think that's very queer indeed," said Pete.
"It is, very," said Willie.
"I mean, whatever way you turn it, I would like to believe ... that what we've doing out here has a reason, to push the Hun back and all that, even if it doesn't have a reason."
"I know," said Willie. But he didn't completely know.
"So what can we call that?"
"I don't know, Pete."
"So where does it leave us?"
...
"Sitting here, Pete, is where," he said.
"Like eejits." And then Pete O'Hara said nothing for a little while. "But I wish they hadn't shot those fellas all the same." It was almost a whisper.
"I wish they hadn't too, Pete," said Willie ... (139)

Shortly after, Willie writes to his father back in Ireland recalling a rebel his own age shot in a Dublin doorway. The ruins of the Belgian town of Ypres, surrounding him, become one with the ruins of Dublin, renamed the New Ypres **[Figure 8]** in the postcard he holds in his hands – both towns mere dots on a vast international map of battles and alliances, treaties and betrayals. Irish, British, German, French. One big mist of global confusion, as mustard gas rolled through the trenches. 1916 was not just Irish politics, it was European geopolitics.

Figure 8 | Sheila Gallagher, *Dublin into Ypres*

It's in retrospect that we divide historical muddles into grand narratives of binary opposition: Irish versus British, Northern versus Southern, unionist versus nationalist. It was *after* the events that the makers of memory imposed neat ideologies on what was often a big puzzle at the time. What are now celebrated as deliberate military campaigns were frequently conducted through foggy dew and swirling smoke. In our lust for simplification we often forget the mess of history. Militarist memorials hide the perplexity of human action and passion.

But if we recall with historian Benedict Anderson that every nation is an "imagined community", we can begin to reimagine 1916 in new ways. Making history is also a matter of remaking it, giving futures to aborted pasts. We need to recollect not only "the terrible beauty" that *was* born but also the still-births, half-births or almost-births that never saw the light of day.

CROSSING BOUNDARIES

The anecdotes related thus far are oral memories, and before moving on to written ones, there's one more tale I would like to record. It's a story I first heard as a pupil growing up in Glenstal Abbey in Ireland, and which was never committed to official history. It simply did not fit.

In 1916 a young Limerick woman, Winifred Barrington, aged twenty-three, was serving in the ambulance corps of the British army in France. While she was nursing soldiers in the trenches, she was also writing postcards home to her rebel friend, Mike Hayes, back in Glenstal **[Figure 9]**. One such card read: "I am looking forward tremendously to returning to Ireland in March. I have been to a few dances and plays, one Irish one was grand. I'll ride up and see you directly I get home, best regards, W.F. Barrington."

Winnie, as she was known, traversed boundaries with abandon, ignoring divisions of class and religion. Growing up in Ireland in conflicted times, she defied convention and daily crossed the road separating her Ascendancy castle from the Catholic laborers of Murroe village. Mike Hayes was her favorite.

In the mornings Winnie brought food to poor families in the hills. Afternoons, she rode to hounds with her Protestant neighbors and dined with loyalist landlords. Evenings, she danced with Mike Hayes and his Fenian friends on the old platform near Abington Bridge.

The Hayes family was well known for its Republican loyalties, but that didn't stop the relationship between Mike and Winnie. And it was reported that on one occasion, when Crown forces captured a tricolor from Mike and were holding it as evidence, Winnie visited the barracks and smuggled the flag out in the folds of her petticoat.

But her close relationship with Mike Hayes didn't prevent her from also befriending Major Henry Biggs, district inspector of a local British brigade. Biggs captured local Irish Republican Army (IRA) men and had them strapped to cars as hostages as he drove through the countryside. But Winifred, we are told, "only saw the good side of the twenty-six-year-old Biggs", forming what one neighbor described as an "inexplicable friendship between two young people". "She had no enemies, she trusted everyone." She thought she could sup with devils and turn them into friends.

One evening, at the height of hostilities, Winnie left Glenstal Castle on her white horse. As she passed through the gates she met her father, Sir Charles, returning from London. He asked her to be careful and be back in time for supper. She also met Mr O'Brien, the gatekeeper, who warned her not to go. O'Brien, a British army veteran, particularly loved Winnie, who cooked for him in his lodge. He guessed where she was going and tried to stop her: "I am a soldier myself but I would not dare to speak to those soldiers across the way." He was referring to Major Biggs and his men. But Winnie replied that, having served in the Great War, she "need fear no one", and rode on.

Later that afternoon Winnie shared tea with British officers at a mansion in Killoscully. And it was while returning in a car driven by Biggs at 7.30 p.m. that they were ambushed by the IRA at Coolboreen Bridge. Among the ambush party were Hayeses, but it was never revealed who actually fired the fatal shot. All we can suppose is that some of the republicans Winnie danced with on Abington Bridge were at Coolboreen Bridge when she expired. There was no trial, no evidence, and no one involved in the attack was prepared to tell the full story; but there are many different versions of what happened that evening.

One account claims that Winnie was dressed in "mannish manner" – jodhpurs and military cap – and was mistaken for Biggs. Another claims she was having a driving lesson from Biggs and was sitting beside him at the wheel and got caught in the crossfire. Yet another says she flung herself across his body to prevent him being shot. One of the ambushers is said to have apologized to the dying Winifred, as she expired

Carte Postale

Correspondance

Hotel du Parc. Cannes
Alpes-Maritimes.
France.
I hope you are all grand & best wishes for 1921. It is very hot out here & lovely scenery but I am looking forward tremendously to returning to Ireland in March.

Adresse

Mike Hayes Esq
Moher
Murroe
Limerick
Irelande

IMP. LEVY FILS & CIE, PARIS

Figure 9 | Postcard from Winnie Barrington to Mike Hayes, 1921

from a bullet through the lung, while another, it's said, put several shots into the body, swearing "the bitch would have lived if she'd kept better company".

No one knows for sure. No one told. But when Winifred was laid out in her castle amidst bouquets of rhododendrons from the Glenstal gardens, there wasn't a soul from the townland, Catholic or Protestant, republican or unionist, who did not attend. Passing through Murroe on her way to the cemetery, all houses were closed and blinds drawn. The bell of the church tolled until the procession passed out of sight. The money and land for the building of the Catholic church had been given by Winifred's Protestant father, Sir Charles, along with the graves where two of the Rebel ambushers were later buried. Though the local Catholic priest refused to have them interred on church grounds, Sir Charles offered his own grave and had it lined with the rhododendrons that had bedecked Winnie's tomb. Winnie's own epitaph reads: "Here lies buried all that could die of Winifred Barrington" **[Figure 10]**.

When Sir Charles left Ireland, inconsolable at the loss of his daughter, his castle was passed on to Benedictine monks. Marking the 1916 centenary, members of Glenstal Abbey recovered a long-buried garden named after Winifred, and there they planted seventeen silver birch trees – sixteen for the executed leaders of 1916 and a seventeenth for Winnie herself, who befriended Irish rebels and British alike. The poet Fanny Howe wrote this inscription: "Winifred means Guenevieve/A white phantom/She crossed boundaries without fear."

Here, once again, it is remarkable how a genuine working through of trauma happens *after the event*. For almost a century the story of Winifred Barrington went unremarked – and when I myself was a pupil at Glenstal in the 1970s, no one spoke of her Lady Garden. Sometimes it takes decades, even centuries, for deep wounds to be worked through. And when such catharsis occurs, it is often – as recent trauma studies show – through the recovery of lost narratives.

A last thought for Winnie Barrington. Were she to return to her garden today, how would she remember 1916? Would she wear a poppy for the Fusiliers she saw into their Belgian graves? An Easter lily for her rebel friends? Or a dark rose for both? Perhaps she would wear all three, reminding us that lilies are symbols of rebirth and that the poppy is not the exclusive preserve of British war remembrance but a symbol first invented by a Canadian poet, John McCrea, for all war-grieving peoples – a practice popularized by French and American women known as the Poppy Ladies. One could imagine Winifred wearing a lily on one collar, a poppy on the other, and a red rose in between, reminding us that roses belong to everyone, from the dark Rosaleen of Celtic poetics to the red rose of England and the Rosa Mystica herself.

Winifred held to a common country that exceeded division into nations. She hoped against hope for a place where enemies might become allies, where hostility might yield to hospitality in a new kind of Ireland – post-nationalist and post-unionist.[7] Winnie paid the price, but her hope remains.

Figure 10 | Sheila Gallagher, *Winnie Barrington*

Here lies
all that could die
Loved

Bean-na-h-Eireann
(THE WOMAN OF IRELAND)
Cramp
Cumann na mBan
Inghinidhe na hEireann.
IRISH GIRLS!
THE IRISH CITIZEN
For Men and Women Equally The Rights of Citizenship; From Men and Women Equally The Duties of Citizenship.
Printed in Ireland on Irish Paper.
DW&M 1390 Hamburg
NATIONAL DEMOCRAT.
DUBLIN, FEBRUARY, 1907.
[ONE PENNY MONTHLY.
CONTENTS:
England Murdered My Husband TERENCE MACSWINEY Will Americans Permit the English Free State to Murder His Sister, Mary MacSwiney
MARY MACSWINEY
The Nationis
A Weekly Review of Irish Thought and Affairs.
THURSDAY, SEPTEMBER 21ST, 1905.
MARY MacSWINEY HEAD OF SINN FEIN
DUBLIN, May 25 (A. P.)—Mary MacSwiney has been elected president of the Sinn Fein executive council in succession to Eamon de Valera.
Cumann na mBan
(THE IRISHWOMEN'S COUNCIL),
Headquarters :—206 Great Brunswick S
IRISHWOMEN, JOIN THE
VOLUNTEER MOVEMENT
AND BECOME MEMBERS OF THE ABOVE ORGANISATIO
First Aid and Ambulance Classes
Reserve Corps of Trained Nurses. Drill and Rifle Practice.
Contribute to our Equipment Fund which has already bought Rifles for the
Search her, she is a spy

IRRECONCILABLES

Let us now turn to written testimonies of "twinsome minds". The work of scholarly and archival recovery has already begun, from Roy Foster's timely revisiting of Ireland's cultural revolution in *Vivid Faces* (2014) to Declan Kiberd and P. J. Mathew's *Handbook of the Irish Revival* (2015), and the pioneering rehabilitation of women's role in the Rising by feminist historians like Margaret Ward, Lucy McDiarmid, and Senia Pašeta among others.

Sibling stories of 1916 were not all about brothers. There were also many sisters whose identities dramatically clashed and crossed. But when I was a boy commemorating the fiftieth anniversary of the Rising, there was little talk of the role played by women. No stamps nor statues, no newspaper tributes nor public memorials. Nor much mention – if any – in the mainstream history books. Yet many bold Irish women ran guns and literary salons, taught in colleges and universities, and wrote essays, books, and journals championing liberation. Some ninety women participated in the rebellion of Easter Week itself, sixty of them members of Cumann na mBan, with weapons training proving a handy match for their male adversaries **[Figure 11]**, as Countess Constance Markiewicz and others proved. Many women rebels – known as the "irreconcilables" – were socially and sexually liberated in ways later erased by Catholic-nationalist hagiography. Prime Minister Éamon de Valera, in cahoots with the Church hierarchy, resolved to rid independent Ireland of its last remaining snake – sex. But the irreconcilables resisted this and other patriarchal repressions, and their irrepressible legacy deserves special mention when reflecting on the Rising.[8]

I

First the Sheehy sisters. Hanna and Mary Sheehy were two feisty "irreconcilables". They embraced 1916 as a radical revolution of mind pointing beyond both British imperialism and tribal provincialism. They were at the forefront of the struggle for women's rights in Ireland: the right to vote, to hold power, to own property, to have basic health care and sexual freedom. A struggle they shared with a number

Figure 11 | Sheila Gallagher, *Women of 1916*

of other leading Irish women activists and artists, including figures such as Eva Young, Kathleen Lynch, and the brilliant poet Eva Gore Booth, who dared embrace "romantic sisterhood" in puritanical times.

Hanna and Mary were extremely active writing for cutting-edge journals such as *An Phoblacht*, *Bean na hÉireann* and the *Irish Citizen*. Hanna co-authored the *National Democrat*, a review that defied both British and ecclesiastical authorities, and resolved to find an international readership for its radical mix of socialism and feminism. Mary, for her part, was engaged in spreading new cosmopolitan ideas in the *Nationist*, which boldly championed Ireland's place in Europe and the world. These avant-garde journals were very much in tune with what their friends James Joyce and John Ingleton called a "new movement of human *mind* in Ireland" – one that construed Irish–British relations in global terms and resolved, in James Joyce's words, "to Europeanise Ireland and Hibernicize Europe". The Sheehys refused the sectarian practice of a Catholic parliament for a Catholic people (south of the border) and a Protestant parliament for a Protestant people (north of it).

The sisters' cosmopolitanism was also reflected in their choice of lovers: Hanna chose the pacifist socialist Francis Skeffington, who insisted on taking her name – something very unusual at the time – and was executed by the British while trying (unarmed) to stop violent looting during the Rising. Mary chose the poet internationalist Tom Kettle, who died tragically in the trenches of Flanders.

Both sisters remained active in the post-revolutionary period. Mary pursued her feminist struggle at the level of local government, while waging a campaign for a return to the Proclamation of 1916: "Why not fall back on the classic simplicity of the language of the Proclamation", she wrote to one national newspaper, "that is unequivocal and will satisfy all women?" Hanna, for her part, continued to share cigarettes and egalitarian views on labor and women's rights with other "irreconcilables", and, though she opposed the Treaty of 1921, bravely broke with "the Chief", Éamon de Valera, dismissing him as "essentially conservative and church-bound, anti-feminist, bourgeois ... enamored of abstractions" (Ward 316).

Independent Ireland, both sisters believed, was betraying the great promise of 1916 by introducing a deadly puritanism. A new national censorship was banning important books on sexual health, as well as works by some of Ireland's most innovative writers (over sixteen hundred books were banned between 1922 and 1944); meanwhile, de Valera's constitution was relegating women to what Mary called a permanent "invalidism as the weaker sex", turning Ireland into a "Catholic statelet under Rome's grip". (It was – to take just one example – illegal for single women to rent apartments in Dublin.) Hanna remained an uncompromising radical to the end, founding the Women's Social and Progressive League, and presenting her son Owen with a banned book on contraception on his wedding day! Fifty years before contraceptives were made legal. She died "an unrepentant pagan" in Dublin in 1946.

Despite their anger at the betrayal of 1916, the Sheehy sisters never abandoned the cause of women in Ireland. Their writings today read like clarion calls to later generations. They would surely have rejoiced to see the liberalization of contraception and the passing of recent Irish referenda on divorce and gay marriage, while aware of how far there is still to go. These women remind us that Ireland without its "irreconcilables" will never be fully free.

II

If the Sheehys were amongst the most radical women of 1916, the MacSwineys were not far behind, though this time we are talking sisters-in-law rather than blood sisters. And the sisterhood in question was less than sanguine. Mary and Muriel MacSwiney struggled together in war and peace.

Mary was the sister of poet Terence MacSwiney, the lord mayor of Cork who died on hunger strike in London. She went on to become a leading figure in the republican movement, succeeding de Valera as president of Sinn Féin.

Muriel (née Murphy) was born to a merchant-prince family in Cork, whom she defied by marrying the republican MacSwiney, whose pale-blue eyes and lofty ideals she found irresistible. Though she had doubts about hunger strikes, she stood by her man and, after his death, toured America as an advocate for the republican cause. Muriel also led a campaign for Mary, who had been imprisoned for militant action, displaying placards such as "England murdered my husband, Terence MacSwiney. Will Americans permit the English Free State to murder his sister, Mary?". In 1922 Muriel addressed a meeting in Boston at which she denounced the Church's hostility to Irish republicanism: "We never had the Bishops with us", she informed shocked Bostonians. "Remember in Ireland the Catholic faith ... has nothing to do with religion" (*Boston Daily Globe*, October 1, 1922).

Then came the split **[Figure 12]**. Mary disapproved of Muriel's cosmopolitan lifestyle, and especially her "dissolute" liaison with a Russian communist in Berlin, with whom she had her second child. Indeed, the enmity became so bitter that Mary actually abducted Muriel's daughter in Germany in 1934 and brought her back to Ireland to raise her as a good Catholic girl. There are few records of the "kidnap" (as Muriel called it), most reports being hearsay – something not untypical of the blurring of history and story when matters become too intimate to relate. Though both were deeply republican, when it came to matters of faith and morals the hostility between Mary and Muriel was implacable.

There is little doubt that Mary was jealous of Muriel, disapproving of her marriage to Terence and vying with her over his legacy, especially when it came to religion. While Mary remained a loyal Catholic, Muriel vehemently rejected the Church – part of a general repudiation of the old "Irish pieties" of myth and martyrdom. A

Figure 12 | Kevin Sweet, *Muriel and Mary MacSwiney - The Split*

professed atheist, Muriel had no time for clerical authority or ritual blood sacrifice – a real blow to Mary, who revered Terence's martyrdom as a dying "for Ireland's resurrection" (Foster 318 fn.).

One can only wonder how different things might have been if rebels like Mary and Muriel had not fallen out. How might Ireland look today if Mary's reverence for tradition had accommodated Muriel's desire for liberation? If Catholic nationalism had been more hospitable to secular internationalism rather than retreating back into itself? If Sinn Féin – "ourselves alone" – had spelled mature responsibility rather than isolationist fear? What if martyrdom had been honored more as genuine fraternity than as militarist costume drama and morbid necrophilia? How many more martyred bones have to be dug up and reburied? Could they not rest in peace?

It is very unfortunate that the Marys and Muriels of the Irish psyche became adversaries rather than allies. But things are changing in Ireland today, with more and more women reclaiming their unfinished histories – culturally, socially, politically. And they have no illusions that, one hundred years after the Rising, there's still huge work to be done.

POET SOLDIERS

For the remainder of this essay we recall some rebels whose full "personal" stories went largely untold. The figures we choose – Childers, Casement, and Ledwidge – were all visionaries whose secret dreams and desires were for too long forgotten and deserve to be retrieved [Figure 13].

Figure 13 | **Left-right: Francis Ledwidge, Erskine Childers, Roger Casement**

Genuine commemoration means attending not only to what happened but also to what did not. The past is not just what has passed but what lives on in memory thanks to arrows of futurity that misfired or whose trajectory was interrupted. As philosopher Paul Ricoeur reminds us, history is more than what has taken place and cannot be changed – it equally involves *potential* futures still dormant in the past. It is especially the founding events of a community that require reimagining, at critical moments, in order to unlock their unfinished possibilities. Historical memory involves a return not just to moments of military glory but to dreams forfeited by history. It signals a work of *anticipatory* remembering.

So revisiting these final stories, we might ask again: how do we distinguish between good and bad commemoration? How to differentiate between what Freud called the healing work of "mourning" and the pathology of "melancholy"? Between remembering backwards (addicted to repetition compulsion) and remembering forwards (alert to futures of the past)? In short, how do we tell the difference between memories that incarcerate and memories that emancipate?

I

Let's recall the "twinsome" pair of Erskine Childers and Robert Barton. Double cousins, they grew up surrounded by oak forests in Glendalough, County Wicklow before serving in the British army, and then – radically disillusioned – joining the rebels. How did this happen and what do their stories have to say to us today?

Robert Barton was educated in England and became a British officer at the outbreak of the First World War. Stationed in Dublin during the Rising, he guarded rebels at Richmond Barracks, and was so shocked by the brutal suppression of the Rising that he resigned from the British army. He joined the Irish republicans, and was arrested by the British for sedition. On St Patrick's Day he escaped from Mountjoy Jail, leaving a note for the governor in which he explained that, due to the discomfort of his cell, he felt obliged to leave in a hurry and hoped his luggage could be sent on! Barton was part of the Irish delegation – which included Michael Collins – that signed the Anglo-Irish Treaty of 1921.[9]

His cousin Erskine Childers also joined the British forces – fighting in the Boer War in Africa and in the First World War – before being converted to Irish republicanism. Together with his wife Molly, he ran German guns to Irish nationalists aboard their yacht, the *Asgard*, though this did not stop fellow republican Arthur Griffith from describing him as a "damned Englishman". Erskine also took part in the Treaty negotiations, but broke with Robert when refusing to sign, siding with de Valera over Collins.

Though Erskine was as much writer as partisan, he was arrested after Collins's assassination and sentenced to death for carrying a gun. Ironically, it was a small pistol given him by Collins when they were on the same side before the Treaty – "to keep him safe from enemies". In his last days in prison, Erskine was reconciled with Robert, and even asked his own son to find everyone who had signed his death warrant and shake their hands. Erskine showed extraordinary forgiveness by shaking hands with the members of his own firing squad one by one, his last words to them being, "Take a step forwards lads. It's easier that way."

Robert Barton, as minister for agriculture in the first Irish government in 1919, proposed that the 1916 martyrs be commemorated not with triumphal monuments but with birch trees planted in spring ground. Ireland's first radical ecologist – we might call him – put country before nation, nature before nationalism. His recommendation went unheeded, alas, and he became so disillusioned with civil-war bitterness that he left politics for good. He had an ancestral love of trees, and the sequoia planted at his birth fell in a storm the year he died. It would take almost a century before his idea inspired monks at Glenstal Abbey to plant the seventeen birches in Winifred's garden.

Barton and Childers, despite the split over the Treaty, were two immensely original minds, prepared to change armies and uniforms when compassion and justice demanded. They both had exceptional imaginations – Erskine more literary (authoring the best-selling novel *Riddle of the Sands* **[Figure 14]**), Robert more ecological (celebrating his country's natural resources and landscape). Think how Ireland might have benefitted from their intelligences had Erskine not been egregiously executed and Barton not left politics. One can only imagine – and regret the loss.

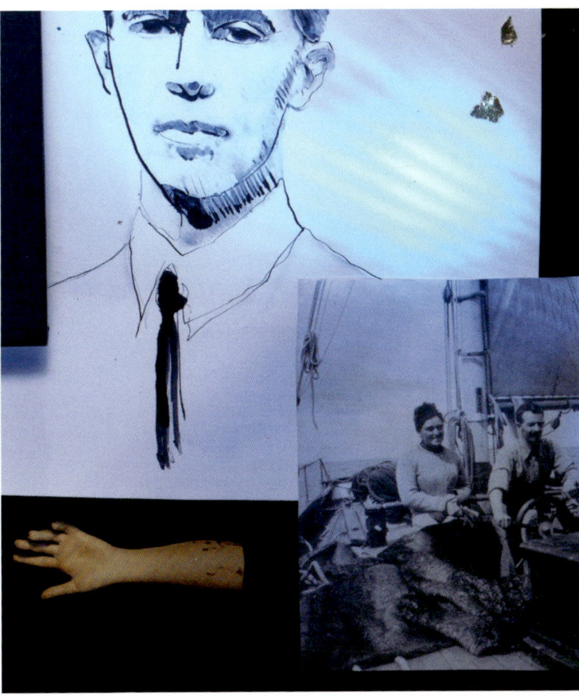

Figure 14 | Sheila Gallagher, *Childers and Barton*

II

Another Irishman who changed uniforms and whose "full" story was hidden for decades is Roger Casement. Though a famous martyr of 1916, part of his life was hushed up for almost a century – namely his love for a man called Millar Gordon. This relationship between nationalist and unionist only came to light in 1998 thanks to historian Jeffrey Dudgeon, who discovered a secret letter written just days before Casement's execution. The document, dated May 1916, confirms the existence of a "mysterious lover" alluded to in Casement's diaries.[10]

In 1916 Millar Gordon worked as a twenty-six-year-old bank clerk and lived in south Belfast, where he often received Casement. His identity was first revealed by a British agent who tracked down the lovers via a Triumph motorbike that Casement purchased for Gordon for £25. The agent sent his memo to Sir Ernley Blackwell, legal adviser to the British Home Office, four days before Casement was hanged for enlisting German support in the Rising. The note remained secret until 1998.

Casement was a remarkable crusader for human rights and a staunch critic of colonialism. His deep indignation at the unforgivable role played by the British government in the Irish famines was no doubt a key incentive for his campaigns against the crimes of empire. A seasoned internationalist, he traveled throughout Europe, Africa, and Latin America, and spent many years – as a consular officer – investigating genocidal abuses in the Amazon region and Congo. Here he revealed the "heart of darkness" at work against defenseless indigenous peoples enslaved for imperial profit. He was knighted for his services and was on personal terms with five members of the British War Cabinet. None of which helped when it came to the verdict.

Curiously, the 1916 memo was never cited in the campaign against Casement, and I strongly suspect the reason is that it revealed a serious and sustained relationship with a real "living person from Belfast". It is certainly revealing how both British and Irish governments responded to Casement's "Black Diaries" – the British vehemently affirming their "degeneracies", the Irish vehemently denying them. But what neither British nor Irish officials could ever contemplate was that the relationship between Casement and Gordon was real and enduring – what Oscar Wilde called "the love that dare not speak its name". Numerous gifts and letters have been recovered, showing deep affection between the two.

Yet another indication of the seriousness of the connection was the manner in which Casement engaged Gordon politically. Though Gordon was a committed unionist when they met, Casement writes proudly to his sister of "a Presbyterian Belfast youth I've turned into a truculent Home Ruler. Read and burn. He is a decent soul."[11]

Though Gordon began as a loyalist who signed the pro-British Ulster Covenant, it did not prevent him having an amorous liaison with someone considered a traitor to Britain and who sought arms from Germany. Casement himself was, it seems, as tormented about his sexual relations as he was about Anglo-Irish ones – how could he live his forbidden sexuality freely? How, as a British knight, could he free Ireland? Questions he asked during his grueling visit to the Western Front mired in the international theater of war. But he did find a moment of calm towards the end. After his failed landing of arms from a German U-boat in Kerry on Good Friday 1916, Casement had a kind of epiphany. Disillusioned with his idealized Germans, unhappy with the timing of the rebellion, and exhausted from countless British betrayals and conspiracies, Casement suddenly let go of all anxiety and, awaiting arrest, lay down in the sand. He listened to the birdsong, feeling at peace for the first time in years:

Although I knew that this fate waited on me, I was for one brief spell happy and smiling once more. I cannot tell you what I felt. The sand hills were full of skylarks, rising in the dawn – the first sound I heard through the surf was their song as I waded in through the breakers, and they kept rising all the time up to the old rath at Currahane ... and all round were primroses and wild violets and the singing of skylarks in the air, and I was back in Ireland again (cited in Foster 239).

Casement was a deeply contested figure both before and after the Rising. Originally hailed by the British as a crusader for human rights, he was reviled for treason once he espoused the republican cause. Likewise, revered as a martyr by many Irish republicans, he was accused by some as knowing "nothing about Ireland since he was all the time out of it". Not for the first time, an actor of 1916 fell foul of both sides – loyalist and nationalist, British and Irish, Protestant and Catholic (Casement converted to Catholicism at the end). In many ways, Casement – like his compatriot Ernest Shackleton, whose 1916 expedition to the Antarctic went largely unsung – was considered too Irish in England and too English in Ireland. A double outsider. A constant contradiction. Casement transgressed all boundaries – national, sexual, political, religious – and paid the price.

As for Millar Gordon, we have no definitive records. All we know is that in 1920, four years after Casement's execution, Millar Gordon crossed the border from Ulster to Dublin, where he died in 1956. What his last thoughts on his lover were we can only imagine, but he was surely not unaware of Yeats's haunting lines:

> *O what has made that sudden noise?*
> *What on the threshold stands?*
> ...
> *What gave that roar of mockery,*
> *That roar in the sea's roar?*
>
> *The ghost of Roger Casement*
> *Is beating on the door.*
> (from "The Ghost of Roger Casement") **[Figure 15]**

Figure 15 | Sheila Gallagher, ***The Ghost of Roger Casement***

III

To end, we recall the story of the poet soldier Francis Ledwidge – another brilliant mind caught in the crossfire of British–Irish relations. A Catholic laborer from Meath, Ledwidge sided with the Irish Volunteers before enlisting in the British army. He was, like many, persuaded by Redmond that fighting with Britain would help achieve Home Rule, declaring that "he could not stand aside while others sought to defend Ireland's freedom".

Ledwidge was killed at Boesinghe, Flanders in July 1917. It was the first day of the third Battle of Ypres, and he was serving with the Royal Inniskilling Fusiliers. Aged twenty-nine, he was having a tea break when struck by German artillery. He fell at a place called Le Carrefour de la Rose (Crossroads of the Rose). A chaplain who knew him, Father Devas, recorded: "Ledwidge killed, blown to bits."

Today Ledwidge's grave is inscribed with lines from his poem "Lament for Thomas McDonagh", a signatory of the 1916 Proclamation whose violent death in Dublin prefigured Ledwidge's own. Ledwidge and MacDonagh may have worn opposite uniforms, but they were brothers at heart:

He shall not hear the bittern cry
in the wild sky, where he is lain.
Nor voices of the sweeter birds
Above the wailing of the rain.[12]

In another poem from Flanders **[Figure 16]**, "Lament for the Poets of 1916", Ledwidge confessed empathy for the dreams of the Dublin "martyrs" at a time when Ireland oscillated between being a country and nation. If *nation* is construed as a unitary political ideal, *country* is a place of natural elements and multiple living things – birds, flora, rivers, trees, people. Assuming the voice of the Poor Old Woman (icon of Ireland mourning her sons), Ledwidge gives her a concrete locale, "Derry of the little hills":

...
"At break of day the fowler came
and took my blackbirds from their songs
who loved me well thro' shame and blame
...
But in the lovely hush of eve
Weeping I grieve the silent hills."

Ledwidge blends images of his own childhood in Meath with symbols of the martyrs whom the woman mourns as vanished birds she hopes one day will return. Ledwidge sees blackbirds as liminal creatures, half natural and present, half symbolic and absent – double denizens of Ireland as a "country" that exists and a "nation" yet to exist.

Figure 16 | Sheila Gallagher, *Flanders*

Sixty years on, Irish Nobel Laureate Seamus Heaney composed a powerful elegy to Ledwidge. Written in 1980, at the height of the Ulster Troubles, Heaney recognizes a mirror image in this conflicted poet. He reimagines Ledwidge forlorn in the trenches, which Heaney compares to passage graves of the Boyne, where Ledwidge grew up. Heaney quotes a letter from Ledwidge lamenting his split between the Britain he serves in Flanders and the Ireland he has left behind with no "place among the nations but the place of Cinderella". Confessing deep inner division, Ledwidge expresses hope for some post-war reunion: "I am sorry that party politics should ever divide our own tents but not without the hope that a new Ireland will arise from her ashes in the ruins of Dublin, like the Phoenix, with one purpose." Heaney enters the mind of Ledwidge thus:

I think of you in your Tommy's uniform,
A haunted Catholic face, pallid and brave,
Ghosting the trenches with a bloom of hawthorn
Or silence cored from a Boyne passage-grave.
...
But a big strafe puts the candles out in Ypres:
...
"To be called a British soldier while my country
Has no place among nations ..."

Heaney locates Ledwidge's identity crisis in the double culture he grew up in, playing nationalist Gaelic games with locals and cricket with his unionist mentor Lord Dunsany: writing his best poem for a 1916 martyr while having his first volume introduced by a loyalist peer. Heaney concludes his elegy by identifying these "strains" of crossed loyalty as both a conflict in Irish–British politics *and* a cleft in Ledwidge's own psyche: a double split that tore him to shreds as brutally as the shrapnel from German guns.

You were rent
By shrapnel six weeks later ...
...
In you, our dead enigma, all the strains
Criss-cross in useless equilibrium
...
You were not keyed or pitched like these true-blue ones
Though all of you consort now underground.
(from "In Memoriam Francis Ledwidge")

Heaney imagines different soldiers marching to different tunes, all reconnected through the underground passage graves joining Boyne to Boesinghe. And, curiously, it is to a similar Boyne connection that Frank McGuinness alludes in his play *Observe the Sons of Ulster Marching Towards the Somme* (1985), where a troupe of Northern Protestants prepare for battle. Facing the River Somme on July 1 – the date their forefathers waged the Battle of the Boyne in 1690 – the Ulstermen reimagine all the Irish rivers they have left behind: "Jesus, that's it. The source of that strange smell. The river ... the Somme ... It smells like home. A river at home ... It's bringing us home. We're not in France ... This river is ours. This land's ours. We've come home ... The Somme, it's not what we think it is. It's the Lagan, the Foyle, the Bann."

CONCLUDING

Heaney, McGuinness, Callaghan, Barry, Howe – all these and many other Irish writers have been responding to 1916 with stories that supplement history. Working across generations, they transmute trauma into drama to the extent that intolerable pain calls for conversion into narrative if healing is to occur. Trauma, Freud taught us, refers to "wounds" so deep they cannot be processed at the time and require a later "working through" in images and words – *after* the event, *nachträglich*. Regarding 1916 – no less than the Famine and other violent ruptures in Ireland's past – the metamorphosis of history into story achieves catharsis by turning ghosts into ancestors. The ghosts of 1916 must be laid so that living men and women may return – each with its "local habitation and a name". That is what Sheila Gallagher and I try to gesture at in our interplay of word and image: an experiment we hope contributes in some way to the ongoing revival of the unfinished revivals of 1916.

Good commemoration, we believe, offers a way beyond pathological polarities of either/or towards an open culture of *both/and* **[Figure 17]**. The centenary offered a chance to transcend the clash of binaries – nationalist or unionist, poppy or lily, Protestant or Catholic – so that Ireland and Britain might escape cycles of enmity and become players on a more transnational stage (regional, European, global). This maturation beyond mimetic rivalry is helped, we suggest, by embracing an Ireland the poets and artists have imagined: a nation more wisely balanced "between" country and cosmos.

Country, as noted, marks a commons of earth and elements: a shared ecology of lands and waters. Recall Barton's birches, Ledwidge's blackbirds, McGuinness's rivers, Winifred's flowers and forests of remembrance. Think also of Heaney's underground passageways and bottomless bogs that open onto oceans:

> *That subject people stuff is a cod's game*
>
> ...
>
> ... *It's time to swim*

out on your own and fill the element
with signatures on your own frequency,
echo soundings, searches, probes, allurements,

elver-gleams in the dark of the whole sea.
(from 'Station Island', section XII)

Country is a place of body and flesh **[Figure 18]**, of brotherhood and sisterhood (Barton and Childers, the Sheehys and MacSwineys); it's a place of daring desire and yay-saying life (Casement and Gordon, Muriel MacSwiney and her men, Winnie Barrington and hers); it is a promise of unfailing natality, which precedes the nation and seeds its reinvention.

But if country marks a space *before* the nation, there's also a space *beyond* it – and it goes by the name of *cosmos*. This is a site that transcends all frontiers – a fifth province of mind that exceeds the four provinces of north, south, east, and west. It is the Finistère of hope where all pilgrimages lead, going back to the *navigatios* of ancient Irish monks – diasporas of risk allowing for new possibilities of thought. Such a migrant cosmos was, we believe, a catalyst of the great cultural enlightenment that ignited a whole revolution of ideas in the extraordinary generation of 1916. It promised a genuinely pluralist vision witnessed in the proliferation of Revivalist writings and journals in the first quarter of the twentieth century. Brilliant imaginative work ranging from the 1916 leaders themselves – Pearse, Connolly, and Griffith all edited their own intellectual journals – to the bold cosmopolitanism of Kettle and the Sheehys. Utopian vision vowed to international emancipation and the regeneration of mind announced by James Joyce – one where everyone could say *Mundanus sum*, I belong to the world.

Figure 17 | Sheila Gallagher, *Poppy Lily Rose*

Figure 18 | Sheila Gallagher, *Woman of the Hills*

This cosmos of imagination is a privileged site for the remaking of symbols – as we have tried to indicate in our criss-crossing scenes of bridges and trenches, of river runs and passageways, between Boyne and Boesinghe, Dublin and Ypres, the Lagan and the Somme. Exchanging stories, changing histories. Recovering and reinventing again and again.

So let us end with rivers that never end, and one river in particular on whose banks the Dublin Four Courts and General Post Office rose up and fell in 1916, and from whose quays and harbors naval ships sailed to Flanders full of Royal Irish Fusiliers. A river that served as a waterway for centuries, opening Ireland to the world and the world to Ireland – visitors and invaders, migrants and planters, aliens and refugees; not to mention the boatloads of Famine survivors escaping to Liverpool, London, Glasgow, and beyond. The same river crossed by canals where the Irish poet, Paddy Kavanagh, composed his memorial to the quotidian and the banal: "O commemorate me with no hero-courageous/Tomb – just a canal bank seat for the passer-by" **[Figure 19]**. The river that Joyce turned into Anna Livia, bringer of plurabilities, whose music "rendered all animated greatbritish and Irish" things visible in its "glistery gleam darkling adown surface of affluvial flowandflow" (*Finnegans Wake*, 1939). "Mememormee, mememormee", the Joycean washerwomen chimed until, retelling history and forgiving the past, they could say "lave it so".

"Lave it so." As in "laver", to wash and heal the wounds of the past. And also as in "let be": we'll leave it, so. For too much remembrance, as Friel reminds us, is a form of madness. There are times to reclaim and times to let go. The year 1916 is a time for both. Remembering and forgetting in right balance is a way of salving the scars of the past. Forgetting what's been too remembered – the grand triumphal myths – and remembering what's too forgotten – the promissory notes, the ordinary acts of audacity and empathy. History is in between. Ireland needs a healing of history through a catharsis of story. The work of recreation goes on.

ENDNOTES

[1] On this notion of anticipatory memory as a retrieval of the future of the past, see Ricoeur, *Memory, History and Forgetting*, and Carr and Taylor, "Ricoeur on Narrative", 160–87.

[2] See for example James Connolly: "Providence sent the potato blight but England made the Famine ... We are sick of the canting talk of those who tell us that we must not blame the British people for the crime of their rulers against Ireland. We do blame them"; cited by Joseph O'Connor in his Irish Famine novel *Star of the Sea* (London: Random House, 2004), 2.

[3] On the notion of trauma as "unexperienced experience", see Ivor Browne, "Unassimilated happenings", in idem, *The Writings of Ivor Browne*, and Kearney, "Writing trauma", 131–44.

[4] These citations are further analyzed in our essays "Myth and motherland" and "The triumph of failure", in Richard Kearney, *Navigations: Collected Irish Essays, 1977–2007* (Dublin and Syracuse, NY: Lilliput Press/Syracuse University Press, 2009).

[5] On the work of commemoration and representation in relation to 1916, see Wills, *Dublin 1916*, and in relation to the Famine, see O'Sullivan, *The Tombs of a Departed Race*, and Gibbons, *Limits of the Visible*. On the therapeutic "work of memory", see Ricoeur, "Memory and forgetting", 5–11.

[6] On transgenerational trauma as a "failure of witnessing" and the need for narrative remembrance and restorative catharsis, see my "The ethics of narrative remembrance", in Kearney and Dooley (eds), *Questioning Ethics*, 18–32; "Memory in Irish culture: an exploration", in Oona Frawley (ed.), *Memory Ireland: The Famine and the Troubles*, vol. 3 (Syracuse, NY: Syracuse University Press, 2014), 138–51; and "Narrating pain: the power of catharsis", in Richard Bégin and Lucie Roy (eds), *Figures de la Violence: Collections Esthétiques* (Paris: L'Harmattan, 2011).

[7] See Kearney, *Postnationalist Ireland*, and the ongoing work of the Guestbook peace project, launched in Glenstal Abbey in July 2009 (see http://www.guestbookproject.org). I am indebted to Glenstal historians Anthony Keane OSB and Brian Murphy OSB for many of the local stories and memories of Winifred Barrington.

[8] On the key role of women "irreconcilables" in 1916, see Roy Foster's chapter "Lovers", in idem, *Vivid Faces*, 75 ff., and Margaret Ward's biography, *Hanna Sheehy Skeffington*. See also Foster's dramatic portrayal of Min and Mary Kate Ryan, sibling sisters who found themselves on opposite sides during the Anglo-Irish Treaty debates and subsequent civil war.

[9] I am indebted to Fanny Howe and Roy Foster for their insights into the Barton-Childers relationship.

[10] See Dudgeon, *Roger Casement*. I am indebted to Dudgeon's pioneering research.

[11] See Foster on Casement, *Vivid Faces*, 138–9.

[12] See Ledwidge, *The Ledwidge Treasury*. There was a renewal of interest in the long-neglected life and work of Ledwidge for the 2016 commemoration, marked by several radio and television documentaries in the Irish and British media, and a graphic book of his life, *Francis Ledwidge: Ireland's Soldier Poet*, Teaching Histories Project (Derry: The Nerve Centre, 2016).

WORKS CITED

Barry, Sebastian. *A Long Way Home.* London: Penguin, 2005.

Browne, Ivor. "Unassimilated happenings". *The Writings of Ivor Browne*. Cork: Atrium Press, 2013.

Carr, David, Charles Taylor and Paul Ricoeur. "Ricoeur on narrative". *On Paul Ricoeur: Narrative and Interpretation*. David Wood, ed. London: Routledge, 1991.

Dudgeon, Jeffrey. *Roger Casement: The Black Diaries.* Belfast: Belfast Press, 2002.

Foster, R. F. *Vivid Faces.* London and New York: W. W. Norton & Co, 2014.

Friel, Brian. *Translations: A Play.* New York: Samuel French, Inc, 1981.

Gibbons, Luke. *Limits of the Visible: Representing the Great Hunger.* Hamden, CT: Quinnipiac University Press, 2014.

Heaney, Seamus. *The Redress of Poetry.* New York: Farrar, Straus & Giroux, 2011.

---. *Seamus Heaney: Selected Poems, 1966–1987.* New York: Farrar, Straus & Giroux, 1990

Higgins, Michael D. "Reflecting on the Gorta Mór: the Great Famine of Ireland". In idem, ed. *When Ideas Matter: Speeches for an Ethical Republic*. London: Head Zeus, 2016.

Kearney, Richard. "The ethics of narrative remembrance". In idem and Mark Dooley, eds. *Questioning Ethics*. London: Routledge, 1999.

---. "Memory in Irish culture: an exploration". In Oona Frawley, ed. *Memory Ireland: The Famine and the Troubles*, vol. 3. Syracuse, NY: Syracuse University Press, 2014.

---. "Myth and motherland". In idem, *Navigations: Collected Irish Essays, 1977–2007*. Dublin: Lilliput Press/Syracuse, NY: Syracuse University Press, 2009.

---. "Narrating pain: the power of catharsis". In Richard Bégin and Lucie Roy, eds. *Figures de la Violence: Collections Esthétiques*. Paris: L'Harmattan, 2011.

---. *Postnationalist Ireland.* London: Routledge, 2002.

---. "The triumph of failure." In idem, *Navigations: Collected Irish Essays, 1977–2007*. Dublin: Lilliput Press/Syracuse, NY: Syracuse University Press, 2009.

---. "Writing trauma: narrative catharsis in Homer, Shakespeare and Joyce". In Bandy Lee, Nancy Olson and Thomas P. Duffy, eds. *Making Sense: Beauty, Creativity and Healing*. New York: Peter Lang Publishing, 2015.

Kiberd, Declan and P. J. Mathews, eds. *Handbook of the Irish Revival*. Dublin: Abbey Theatre Press, 2016.

Lawless, Emily. "Famine roads and Famine memories (1898)". In Declan Kiberd and P. J. Mathews, eds. *Handbook of the Irish Revival: An Anthology of Irish Cultural and Political Writings, 1891–1922*. Dublin: Abbey Theatre Press, 2016.

Ledwidge, Francis. *The Ledwidge Treasury: Selected Poems.* Dublin: New Island Books, 2007.

Ó Faoláin, Seán. *An Irish Journey*. London: Longmans, Green & Co., 1941.

O'Sullivan, Niamh. *The Tombs of a Departed Race: Illustrations of Ireland's Great Hunger.* Hamden, CT: Quinnipiac University Press, 2014.

Ricoeur, Paul. "Memory and forgetting". In Richard Kearney and Mark Dooley, eds. *Questioning Ethics*. London and New York: Routledge, 1999.

---. *Memory, History and Forgetting.* Chicago: Chicago University Press, 2004.

Ward, Margaret. *Hanna Sheehy Skeffington: A Life*. Dublin: Attic Press, 1997.

Wills, Clair. *Dublin 1916.* Cambridge, MA: Harvard University Press, 2009.

IMAGES

Cover

Hughie O'Donoghue
b. 1953
On Our Knees
1996/1997
Acrylic on canvas
40 x 60 in (101.6 x 152.4 cm)
© Hughie O'Donoghue

Figure 1

Sheila Gallagher
Twinsome Minds: Ferdia and Cuchulain
2016
After Louis le Brocquy illustration for *The Tain*, trans. Thomas Kinsella (Dublin: Dolman Press, 1969)
Ink collage on paper
14.2 x 11 in (36 x 28 cm)

Figure 2

Sheila Gallagher
From the Graves Spring
2017
Collage and projection on paper
22 x 18.1 in (56 x 46 cm)

Figure 3
1916 commemoration scrapbook (fiftieth anniversary, 1966)
From the collection of Richard Kearney

Figure 4

Pádraig Pearse 1966 commemorative coin
www.irishcoinage.com (accessed January 16, 2017)

Figure 5

Sheila Gallagher
Same Wool
Presentation still from performance of *Twinsome Minds*, 2016

Figure 6

Sheila Gallagher
Eoin Callaghan's Plane
Projection still from performance of *Twinsome Minds*, 2016
Photograph by Stewart Clements

Figure 7

Irish Volunteers and First World War recruitment posters

Figure 8

Sheila Gallagher
Dublin into Ypres
2016
Mixed media on paper
22 x 18.1 in (56 x 46 cm)

Figure 9

Postcard from Winnie Barrington to Mike Hayes, 1921
Originally reproduced in Brian P. Murphy, *Glenstal Abbey Gardens* (Papaver Editions, 2014)

Figure 10

Sheila Gallagher
Winnie Barrington
Assemblage of objects and images from *Twinsome Minds*, 2016
Photograph by Stewart Clements

Figure 11

Sheila Gallagher
Women of 1916
Source materials from studio of Sheila Gallagher

Figure 12

Kevin Sweet
Muriel and Mary MacSwiney – The Split
2016
Digital collage

Figure 13

Francis Ledwidge, Erskine Childers, Roger Casement
Sources: Francis Ledwidge, c. 1914, George Grantham Bain Collection (Library of Congress); Erskine Childers, Trinity College Archive; Roger Casement, http://centenariestimeline.com

Figure 14

Sheila Gallagher
Childers and Barton
Assemblage of objects and images from *Twinsome Minds*, 2016
Photograph by Stewart Clements

Figure 15

Sheila Gallagher
The Ghost of Roger Casement
Performance still from *Twinsome Minds*, 2017
Photograph by Stewart Clements

Figure 16

Sheila Gallagher
Flanders
2015
Ink on paper
8.7 x 11 in (22 x 28 cm)
Private collection

Figure 17

Sheila Gallagher
Poppy Lily Rose
2016
Video still from *Twinsome Minds*, 2016

Figure 18

Sheila Gallagher
Woman of the Hills
2015
Ink on paper
7.9 x 14.2 in (20 x 36 cm)

Figure 19

Sheila Gallagher
Commemorate Me Where There Is Water
Performance still from *Twinsome Minds*, 2017
Photograph by Stewart Clements

ABOUT THE AUTHORS

Richard Kearney is a professor of philosophy at Boston College and author of many books on Irish thought, literature, and culture, including *Navigations: Collected Irish Essays, 1977–2007* and *Postnationalist Ireland: Philosophy, Poltiics, Culture* (London: Routledge, 1998). He has also published two novels and a volume of poetry. He is co-director, with Sheila Gallagher, of the Guestbook Project for Exchanging Stories.

Sheila Gallagher is an interdisciplinary artist, curator, and professor of art at Boston College. She has had numerous exhibitions at galleries, museums, and universities in the US and internationally, including the Moving Image Festival, London, the Institute of Contemporary Art, Boston, the Museum of Fine Arts, Boston, and Crystal Bridges Museum, Arkansas. Gallagher is co-director of the Becker Archive, the largest private collection of US Civil War drawings.

Figure 19 | Sheila Gallagher, *Commemorate Me Where There Is Water*

SERIES EDITOR

Niamh O'Sullivan

IMAGE RESEARCH

Claire Puzarne

DESIGN

www.rachelfoleydesigns.com

ACKNOWLEDGMENT

Office of Public Affairs, Quinnipiac University

PUBLISHER

Quinnipiac University Press

PRINTING

GRAPHYCEMS

ISBN 978-0-9978374-5-2

Ireland's Great Hunger Museum
Quinnipiac University

3011 Whitney Avenue
Hamden, CT 06518-1908
203-582-6500

www.ighm.org